Above and Beyond Coping

Discovering Resilience,Embracing and Thriving Through Life's Challenges

By

Justin cools

Table of content

Introduction:

Notwithstanding misfortune, it is often our capacity to adapt that determines how we explore through testing circumstances. Survival techniques are significant for managing stressors and difficulties. Be that as it may, there come situations where essentially adapting isn't sufficient. It is during these minutes that we should blow away adapting and dive into the domain of finding flexibility. Versatility encompasses not simply the capacity to quickly return from challenges, but additionally the solidarity to develop, adjust, and flourish even with misfortune. This excursion towards finding versatility is a significant investigation of our internal strength and our persevering quest for self-improvement. In this article, we will dive into the idea of versatility and its importance in our lives.

Furthermore, how can we go beyond simple endurance to uncover our actual likelihood in the midst of difficulties? We will investigate the different elements that add to flexibility, the job of attitude and self-conviction, and reasonable systems that can help us develop and reinforce our versatility.

Chapter 1:

The Force of Flexibility:

Versatility is a strong quality that empowers people to return quickly from difficulty and beat life's difficulties. It's the capacity to adjust and flourish, notwithstanding hardships. Flexibility isn't something you're brought into the world with; it very well may be developed and fortified after some time. Here are a few vital parts of the force of strength:

Close to home Strength: Strong individuals have the ability to successfully deal with their feelings. They recognize their sentiments, yet they don't allow them to overwhelm their direction.

Critical thinking Abilities: Flexibility includes being creative and tracking down answers to issues. Rather than harping on the issue, versatile people center around how they might advance the circumstance.

Hopefulness: Versatile individuals will more often than not keep an uplifting perspective on life, in any event, during difficult stretches. They have faith in their capacity to overcome difficulties and consider mishaps to be open doors for development.

Social Help: Building an encouraging group of loved ones is essential for flexibility. Having individuals to rest on during troublesome times can give profound strength and pragmatic assistance. Adaptability: Versatility requires adaptability and flexibility. Life is loaded with unforeseen turns, and having the option to change your arrangements and objectives is fundamental for quickly returning.

Taking care of oneself: Dealing with your physical and mental prosperity is the key to strength. This incorporates customary activity, a reasonable eating regimen, sufficient rest, and stress management.

Gaining from Misfortunes: Versatile people view mishaps as important growth opportunities. They dissect what turned out badly, make vital changes, and utilize that information to work on it from here on out.

Objective Setting: Defining reachable objectives and pursuing them gives a feeling of motivation and course, which can upgrade versatility.

Keeping up with Viewpoint: Versatile individuals continue to challenge circumstances in context. They advise themselves that difficulty is a piece of life, and it doesn't characterize their whole presence.

Looking for Proficient Assistance: Now and again, flexibility might include looking for proficient direction, like treatment or advice, to adapt to horrendous accidents or progressing battles.

In outline, the force of flexibility lies in its capacity to help people make due as well as flourish even with misfortune. Expertise can be created and sharpened over the long haul, prompting a seriously satisfying and strong life.

Grasping ways of dealing with especially difficult times:

difficulty, or testing circumstances. They can be arranged into different kinds:

Positive survival strategies:

Critical thinking: This includes recognizing the issue, conceptualizing arrangements, and making a move to determine it. Seeking support: discussing your thoughts and looking for help from companions, family, or professionals. Healthy Way of Life: Taking part in customary activities, eating well, and getting sufficient rest can assist with decreasing stress. Mindfulness and Unwinding: Strategies like contemplation, profound breathing, or yoga can advance unwinding and diminish anxiety. Time The board: Coordinating your undertakings and defining boundaries can assist with managing pressure.

Maladaptive survival strategies:

Evasion: overlooking or keeping away from the wellspring of stress, which can prompt long-haul issues. Substance misuse, which involves using medications or liquor to numb close to home, can cause torment and often intensify problems. Denial: declining to recognize an issue exists, preventing the capacity to address it. Escapism: utilizing interruptions like extreme video gaming or marathon watching television to stay away from the real world.

Versatile survival techniques:

Transformation: acclimating to the circumstances, tolerating what can't be changed, and tracking down better approaches to thrive. Humor: Utilizing humor to ease up the temperament and gain viewpoint on challenges Resilience: returning from affliction with newly discovered strength and gaining from setbacks Understanding and utilizing positive survival techniques can advance mental and profound prosperity, while perceiving and tending to maladaptive ones is essential for self-improvement and wellbeing.

Investigating the various kinds of survival techniques: versatile and maladaptive

Ways of dealing with especially difficult times are mental procedures individuals use to oversee pressure, profound agony, or testing circumstances. They can be comprehensively sorted into two kinds: versatile and maladaptive survival strategies.

Versatile survival techniques:

Critical thinking: This includes recognizing the main driver of an issue and finding proactive ways to address it. It's a useful methodology.

Profound Articulation: Communicating feelings through talking, composing, or workmanship can help people cycle and deliver repressed feelings. Seeking Social Help: Imparting worries to companions, family, or care groups can give solace and alternate points of view on a circumstance.

Taking care of oneself: Participating in exercises that advance physical and mental prosperity, like activity, contemplation, or side interests, can lessen stress. Positive Thinking: Zeroing in on sure angles and reexamining negative considerations can work on one's outlook. Maladaptive

Survival strategies:

Evasion: Overlooking or taking off from issues can prompt annoying issues and expand pressure in the long run. Substance Misuse: Going to medications or liquor to numb close-to-home agony is hurtful and can prompt fixation.

Disavowal: Declining to recognize that an issue exists can keep people from looking for help or making important changes. Self-Mischief: Participating in reckless ways of behaving as a method for adapting is perilous and ought to be tended to with proficient help. Escapism: Extreme utilization of interruptions like computer games or marathon watching television to get away from reality can thwart individual growth. Understanding these survival strategies can be critical to advancing emotional well-being and assisting people with finding better ways of managing life's difficulties. It's vital to look for proficient direction while confronting relentless difficulties in adapting.

Inspecting solid and powerful methods for dealing with stress that advance

versatility.;

Flexibility, the capacity to return and adjust notwithstanding misfortune, is a quality that can be sustained and reinforced through sound ways of dealing with stress. These techniques help in overseeing pressure and difficulties as well as advancing long-term, close-to-home prosperity. In this part, we will investigate some solid and compelling survival methods that can add to building versatility.

Looking for social help:

Interfacing with confided-in companions, relatives, or care groups can give a feeling of approval, solace, and understanding.

Sharing worries, feelings, and encounters with others can assist with diminishing the weight and gaining alternate points of view on difficulties.

Solid socially encouraging groups of people can support confidence, cultivate a feeling of having a place, and give reasonable assistance and assets.

Rehearsing Taking care of oneself and stress The executives:

Taking part in exercises that advance taking care of oneself, like normal activity, adequate rest, and a reasonable eating routine,

Rehearsing, taking care of oneself and stressing the board is fundamental for keeping up with general prosperity. Here are a some few articles issues to consider:

Taking care of oneself Everyday practice: Lay out an ordinary taking care of oneself schedule that incorporates exercises you appreciate and that assist you with unwinding. This could incorporate reflection, yoga, perusing, or going for long strolls.

Actual Wellbeing: Focus on your actual wellbeing by eating nutritious dinners, getting sufficient rest, and participating in ordinary activity. Actual prosperity enormously influences your capacity to oversee pressure.

Care and Reflection: Care practices and contemplation can assist you with remaining present and diminishing pressure. They energize unwinding and can work on mental clarity.

Put down stopping points: Figure out how to say no when vital and define limits to safeguard your significant investment. Overcommitting can prompt burnout. Positive social associations: Encircle yourself with strong and positive individuals who inspire you. Social associations can be an extraordinary source of everyday reassurance.

Using time effectively: proficiently deal with your time and focus on undertakings. This can decrease the sensation of being overwhelmed. Hobbies and Interests: Participate in side interests and exercises that give you pleasure and permit you to loosen up. Having interests beyond work or obligations is pivotal.

Unwinding Strategies: Investigate different unwinding methods, like profound breathing activities, moderate muscle unwinding, or aromatherapy. Seek proficient assistance. In the event that pressure becomes unmanageable, consider looking for help from a specialist or guide who spends significant time on the executives or emotional well-being.

Self-Sympathy: Be caring and sympathetic toward yourself. Recall that it's OK to have some time off and focus on your well-being. Remember that taking care of oneself and stressing the board are progressing cycles, and what turns out best for you might advance over the long haul. Tailor your way to deal with your singular necessities and focus on taking care of yourself in your regular routine.

Chapter 2:

Releasing Inward Strength:

Life is loaded with difficulties of all shapes and sizes. From confronting individual misfortunes to managing outside hindrances, our inward strength determines how we explore through these troublesome times. In any case, what precisely is internal strength, and how might we take advantage of it to conquer affliction?

Internal strength is the repository of versatility, assurance, and boldness that exists in every one of us. It is the capacity to deal with difficulties directly, to persist whenever hardship rears its ugly head, and to track down the inspiration to continue to push ahead. Releasing this inward strength is generally difficult; however, expertise can be created and sharpened over the long run.

Releasing internal strength is a profoundly private and engaging excursion. It includes taking advantage of your internal stores of strength, assurance, and self-conviction to defeat difficulties and accomplish your objectives. Here are a few central issues on this theme:

Self-Revelation: Releasing internal strength starts with self-disclosure. It's tied in with figuring out your qualities, interests, and the main thing about you. This mindfulness shapes the establishment for outfitting your inward strength.

Confronting Difficulties: Inward strength frequently arises while confronting affliction. It's during troublesome times that we find our ability to persevere, adjust, and drive forward. These difficulties can be private, expert, or even physical.

Outlook Matters: It is pivotal to develop a positive mentality. Having confidence in your capacities, remaining hopeful, and reevaluating negative considerations can assist you in taking advantage of your internal strength while confronting difficulties.

 Versatility: Flexibility is a vital part of internal strength. It's the capacity to return from difficulty and gain from encounters. Versatile peopleThe essay highlights the significance of self-care, which includes both physical and mental components. and mental components.prosperity is fundamental. Legitimate nourishment, exercise, rest, and stress add to areas of strength for internal strength.

 Encouraging group of people: Encircling yourself with a strong organization of loved ones can give you close-to-home strength during testing times. Sharing your encounters and looking for guidance can be empowering. Setting Objectives: Setting clear, reachable objectives provides you with direction and motivation. Achieving these objectives can support your certainty and inward strength.

Beating Dread: Frequently, dread can keep us down. Standing up to your feelings of dread and getting out of your usual range of familiarity is a strong method for releasing internal strength. Perseverance: The way to progress is seldom direct. It requires tolerance and determination. Inward strength empowers you to continue to push forward in spite of hindrances.

Constant Development: Releasing internal strength is a continuous cycle. It's about consistently creating and developing personally, acquiring astuteness from your encounters, and embracing change. Remember that everybody's excursion to release their inward strength is extraordinary. A profoundly private and enabling cycle can prompt a really satisfying and versatile life.

Building Strength in Testing Times:

Strength is the capacity to return from misfortune, and it's an essential expertise to grow, particularly in testing times. Whether you're confronting individual hardships, a worldwide emergency, or basically the highs and lows of day-to-day existence, building versatility can assist you with exploring these difficulties with more noteworthy strength and flexibility. Here are a few vital procedures to assist you with building versatility:

Develop a Development Outlook: Embrace difficulties as any open doors for development. Rather than view difficulties as disappointments, view them as opportunities for growth. A development mentality permits you to adjust and improve ceaselessly.

Keep an emotionally supportive network. Rest on your companions, family, and local area for help. Interfacing with others can offer close-to-home help and new points of view on your difficulties.

Taking care of oneself: Focus on taking care of oneself to decrease pressure and keep up with physical and mental prosperity. This incorporates ordinary activity, a solid eating regimen, and getting sufficient rest.

Put forth reasonable objectives: Break your objectives into sensible advances. Accomplishing little victories en route can support your certainty and motivation. Practice Care: Care methods, like reflection and profound breathing, can assist you with remaining grounded and lessening tension during troublesome times.

Flexibility: Be available to change and adaptable in your methodology. Life is erratic, and being versatile permits you to acclimate to new circumstances. Problem-Settling Abilities: Foster critical thinking abilities to actually handle difficulties. Recognize the issues, conceptualize arrangements, and make a move.

Positive Self-Talk: Challenge negative considerations and practice self-sympathy. Enjoy the same level of generosity and understanding that you would offer to a friend.

Gain from Misfortune: Ponder past difficulties and what you've gained from them. This can contribute significant knowledge to future versatility.

Look for Proficient Assistance: Assuming you find it trying to adapt to tough spots, make it a point to seek proficient assistance from specialists or counselors. Remember that building flexibility is a continuous cycle. It requires investment and practice to foster these abilities, yet they can have a tremendous effect on the way you explore testing times and come out more grounded on the other side.

The Way to Beating Difficulties:

Beating difficulties requires a blend of versatility, critical thinking abilities, and a positive outlook. Here are a few vital standards to assist you in defeating difficulties:

Outlook Matters: Embrace a development mentality, accepting that difficulties are potential open doors for development as opposed to impossible obstacles. Set clear objectives: Characterize your objectives and what achievement means to you. Having a reasonable bearing will keep you centered.

Separate it: Gap the test into more modest, reasonable assignments. This makes it less overpowering and permits you to follow progress. Learn and adjust: Difficulties frequently accompany significant examples.

Embrace the valuable chance to gain from mishaps and change your methodology in like manner.

Look for Help: Go ahead and request help or direction from coaches, companions, or experts who can give significant bits of knowledge.

Remain Positive: Keeping an inspirational perspective can help you find strength and inspiration during difficult stretches.

Industriousness: Continue onward, in any event, when circumstances become difficult. Many difficulties are overcome through sheer determination. Self-care: Deal with your physical and mental prosperity. A sound body and brain are better prepared to handle difficulties.

Embrace Change: Be adaptable and open to change. In some cases, adjusting to new conditions is the way to overcome difficulties.

Recognize and commend your accomplishments, regardless of how small, to keep motivated on your journey. Remember that conquering difficulties is an interaction. And confronting misfortunes en route is OK. Every hindrance you overcome carries you one bit closer to your objectives.

Investigating the Impact of Individual Differences Certainly! Investigating

The impact of individual contrasts is a wide point that can envelop different fields and subjects. Here is a concise outline of the idea and how it applies in various settings:

Brain research: In brain research, individual contrasts allude to the remarkable attributes and characteristics that make every individual unmistakable. Analysts concentrate on how variables like character attributes,

knowledge, and mental styles impact
conduct, comprehension, and close-to-home
reactions. Understanding individual contrasts
is pivotal in fields like clinical brain research,
where it helps tailor medicines to people.

 Training: In schooling, individual contrasts
assume a huge part in planning successful
educational techniques. Teachers perceive
that understudies have changing learning
styles, capacities, and necessities.
Investigating these distinctions assists
teachers with giving customized guidance,
guaranteeing that all understudies can arrive
at their maximum capacity.

 **Business and Authority: In the corporate
world, understanding**

individual contrasts is crucial for viable
administration and collaboration. Pioneers
who perceive and value different qualities
and characters within their groups can

cultivate a more comprehensive and useful workplace.

 Medical care: In medical services, individual contrasts in hereditary qualities, way of life, and physiology influence how people respond to therapies and mediations. Customized medication plans to fit clinical consideration to every patient's extraordinary qualities to improve results

Humanism and Culture: Individual contrasts additionally shape cultural elements. Factors like culture, childhood, and values can prompt different points of view and ways of behaving inside a general public. Sociologists investigate what these distinctions mean for accepted practices, associations, and clashes.

 Innovation and Information Examination: Individual contrasts can be investigated through large amounts of information and AI. Organizations and associations use information-driven methods to deal with client inclinations and conduct, permitting them to fit items and services to individual consumers. Neuroscience: Neuroscientists concentrate on individual contrasts in cerebrum construction and capability, which can impact different parts of discernment, conduct, and emotional well-being.

Character Exploration: Character brain research centers around individual contrasts in attributes like the Large Five (Receptiveness, Scruples, Extroversion, Pleasantness, and Neuroticism). Specialists investigate what these characteristics mean for different life results and interactions. The impact of individual contrasts is a multi-layered and interdisciplinary area of study that keeps on developing with continuous exploration and mechanical headways. Contingent upon your particular interest or setting, you can dig further into any of these fields to investigate the effect of individual contrasts.

Chapter 3:

Saddling the Force of Emotionally Supportive Networks

Saddling the Force of Help Systems Support frameworks assume a vital role in our lives, giving the establishment to self-awareness, versatility, and achievement. Whether it's in our own or proficient lives, having areas of strength for an organization can have a huge effect on the way we explore difficulties and accomplish our objectives. Here are a few critical viewpoints to consider with regards to bridling the force of emotionally supportive networks:

Daily reassurance: Companions, family, and friends and family frequently act as our essential wellspring of everyday encouragement. They are there to tune in, offer solace, and give support during troublesome times. Developing these connections and being open about our sentiments can reinforce this type of help.

Proficient Help: In the working environment, partners, guides, and managers can offer significant help. They can offer direction, share information, and assist with propelling our professions. Building solid expert connections and looking for mentorship can upgrade our expertly supportive network.

Online People Group: In the computerized age, online networks and gatherings have become strong wellsprings of help. Whether you're looking for guidance on a particular subject or searching for a similar local area, the web offers various chances to interface with other people who share your inclinations and difficulties.

Taking care of oneself: Part of outfitting the force of emotionally supportive networks likewise includes dealing with yourself. Focusing on taking care of oneself, including activity, care, and a solid way of life, can make you stronger and better prepared to give and get support.

Adjusting Giving and Getting: Emotionally supportive networks are equal. It's significant not exclusively to look for help when required, but additionally to offer your help to others when they require it. Building a local area in light of shared help makes a more strong and versatile organization.

Defining Limits: While help is essential, it means a lot to define limits to forestall burnout. Being clear about your cutoff points and discussing them with your encouraging group of people guarantees that you maintain a good arrangement.

Looking for Proficient Assistance: In certain circumstances, particularly while managing emotional well-being difficulties, it is fundamental to look for proficient assistance. Psychological wellness experts can offer specific help and direction.

Emergency Backing: In the midst of an emergency, for example, a catastrophic event or individual misfortune, nearby and public associations frequently offer quick help. Knowing where to go in these circumstances can be lifesaving. Harnessing the force of emotionally supportive networks is tied in with perceiving the worth of human associations, both in all kinds of challenges. Fabricating and sustaining these organizations can fundamentally affect your prosperity and capacity to overcome life's difficulties.

Reinforcing Versatility Through Association:

Reinforcing versatility through association is an influential idea that underlines the significance of building and keeping up with significant connections to improve one's capacity to adapt to life's difficulties. Flexibility alludes to the ability to quickly return from misfortune, and it very well may be sustained and reinforced through different types of association:

Social Help: Keeping up major areas of strength with companions, family, and a steady local area can provide a security net during troublesome times. These connections offer daily encouragement, useful assistance, and a feeling of having a place.

The capacity to understand people at their core: Creating the capacity to appreciate individuals on a deeper level can work on your capacity to interface with others on a more profound level. This incorporates perceiving and dealing with your own feelings as well as understanding and relating to the feelings of others.

Proficient Organizations: Building a strong expert organization can upgrade your strength in the working environment. These associations can offer mentorship, joint effort, potential open doors, and important experiences, assisting you with exploring profession challenges.

Taking care of oneself: association with oneself is similarly significant. Rehearsing taking care of oneself, care, and self-sympathy can fortify your inward flexibility, making it more straightforward to confront outside difficulties.

Local area Contribution: Taking part in local area exercises or chipping in cultivates a feeling of association with a bigger reason, advancing strength by giving a feeling of significance and commitment.

Restorative Connections: As far as some might be concerned, treatment or guidance can be an important type of association that guides in handling injury, overseeing pressure, and working on psychological well-being.

Innovation and Online Entertainment: While innovation can work with associations, it's crucial to use it carefully. Developing authentic, significant internet-based associations as opposed to shallow collaborations can add flexibility.

Social and Profound Associations: For some individuals, interfacing with their social or otherworldly roots can give a feeling of character, reason, and strength in testing times. Overall, reinforcing versatility through association is tied to perceiving the interconnected idea of our lives and cultivating connections that offer help. understanding and a feeling of direction. These associations can assist people in exploring misfortune all the more successfully and returning more grounded.

Chapter 4:

"Flexibility in real life

Embracing life's challenges In this section, we dive into the commonsense use of versatility in our regular routines. Versatility isn't just a characteristic; it's a powerful interaction that can be developed and effectively set in motion. Life throws different difficulties our way, from individual mishaps to proficient obstacles, and the capacity to answer versatilely can make all the difference. Building strong foundations The excursion of flexibility starts by understanding and fortifying the primary aspects: Self-Mindfulness: Know yourself—your assets, shortcomings, and triggers. Mindfulness is the foundation of powerful versatility.Chapter 3:

Saddling the Force of Emotionally Supportive Networks

Saddling the Force of Help Systems Support frameworks assume a vital role in our lives, giving the establishment to self-awareness, versatility, and achievement. Whether it's in our own or proficient lives, having areas of strength for an organization can have a huge effect on the way we explore difficulties and accomplish our objectives. Here are a few critical viewpoints to consider with regards to bridling the force of emotionally supportive networks:

Daily reassurance: Companions, family, and friends and family frequently act as our essential wellspring of everyday encouragement. They are there to tune in, offer solace, and give support during troublesome times. Developing these connections and being open about our sentiments can reinforce this type of help.

 Proficient Help: In the working environment, partners, guides, and managers can offer significant help. They can offer direction, share information, and assist with propelling our professions. Building solid expert connections and looking for mentorship can upgrade our expertly supportive network.

 Online People Group: In the computerized age, online networks and gatherings have become strong wellsprings of help. Whether you're looking for guidance on a particular subject or searching for a similar local area, the web offers various chances to interface with other people who share your inclinations and difficulties.

 Taking care of oneself: Part of outfitting the force of emotionally supportive networks likewise includes dealing with yourself. Focusing on taking care of oneself, including activity, care, and a solid way of life, can make you stronger and better prepared to give and get support.

Adjusting Giving and Getting: Emotionally supportive networks are equal. It's significant not exclusively to look for help when required, but additionally to offer your help to others when they require it. Building a local area in light of shared help makes a more strong and versatile organization.

Defining Limits: While help is essential, it means a lot to define limits to forestall burnout. Being clear about your cutoff points and discussing them with your encouraging group of people guarantees that you maintain a good arrangement.

Looking for Proficient Assistance: In certain circumstances, particularly while managing emotional well-being difficulties, it is fundamental to look for proficient assistance.

Psychological wellness experts can offer specific help and direction.

 Emergency Backing: In the midst of an emergency, for example,

catastrophic event or individual misfortune, nearby and public associations frequently offer quick help. Knowing where to go in these circumstances can be lifesaving. Harnessing the force of emotionally supportive networks is tied in with perceiving the worth of human associations, both in all kinds of challenges. Fabricating and sustaining these organizations can fundamentally affect your prosperity and capacity to overcome life's difficulties.

Reinforcing Versatility Through Association:

 Reinforcing versatility through association is an influential idea that underlines the significance of building and keeping up with significant connections to improve one's capacity to adapt to life's difficulties. Flexibility alludes to the ability to quickly return from misfortune, and it very well may be sustained and reinforced through different types of association:

Social Help: Keeping up major areas of strength with companions, family, and a steady local area can provide a security net during troublesome times. These connections offer daily encouragement, useful assistance, and a feeling of having a place.

The capacity to understand people at their core: Creating the capacity to appreciate individuals on a deeper level can work on your capacity to interface with others on a more profound level. This incorporates perceiving and dealing with your own feelings as well as understanding and relating to the feelings of others.

Proficient Organizations: Building a strong expert organization can upgrade your strength in the working environment. These associations can offer mentorship, joint effort, potential open doors, and important experiences, assisting you with exploring profession challenges.

Taking care of oneself: association with oneself is similarly significant. Rehearsing taking care of oneself, care, and self-sympathy can fortify your inward flexibility, making it more straightforward to confront outside difficulties.

Local area Contribution: Taking part in local area exercises or chipping in cultivates a feeling of association with a bigger reason, advancing strength by giving a feeling of significance and commitment.

Restorative Connections: As far as some might be concerned, treatment or guidance can be an important type of association that guides in handling injury, overseeing pressure, and working on psychological well-being.

Innovation and Online Entertainment: While innovation can work with associations, it's crucial to use it carefully. Developing authentic, significant internet-based associations as opposed to shallow collaborations can add flexibility.

Social and Profound Associations: For some individuals, interfacing with their social or otherworldly roots can give a feeling of character, reason, and strength in testing times. Overall, reinforcing versatility through association is tied to perceiving the interconnected idea of our lives and cultivating connections that offer help.

understanding and a feeling of direction. These associations can assist people in exploring misfortune all the more successfully and returning more grounded.

Chapter 5:

Embracing Change:

Change is an unavoidable piece of life, and how we approach it can have a huge impact on our own and proficient development. Embracing change implies tolerating it as well as considering it a chance for development and innovation. Change as an Impetus for Development: Change frequently pushes us out of our usual range of familiarity, constraining us to adjust and learn. It provokes us to foster new abilities and viewpoints, at last prompting individual and expert development.

Flexibility Even with Change: Strength is a vital characteristic in embracing change. It includes remaining positive and versatile even amidst vulnerability. Developing flexibility assists us with exploring change all the more.

Embracing Change in the Work Environment: In the business world, associations that embrace change will quite often be more coordinated and cutthroat. Representatives who are available to change can drive development and assist organizations with remaining significant in a quickly advancing business sector.

Outlook Matters: A development mentality, instead of a decent attitude, is vital with regards to change. A development mentality considers difficulties to be potential chances to learn and improve, while a proper outlook might oppose change out of dread of disappointment.

Change The board: Change ought to be overseen to actually limit disturbance. This includes clear correspondence, including partners, and offering help and assets to work with a smooth change.

Gaining from Change: Pondering past changes can be sagacious. What worked? Actually, what didn't? These examples can guide future undertakings and assist people and associations in becoming more capable of taking care of progress.

Embracing Individual Change: On an individual level, embracing change implies being open to new encounters, connections, and self-awareness. It's tied in with getting out of your usual range of familiarity to investigate the unknown. In the end, embracing change isn't just about adapting to it; it's tied in with flourishing in an always-impacting world. By fostering a positive mentality, building versatility, and gaining from our encounters, we can transform change into a strong power for development and improvement in our lives and work environments.

Adjusting and flourishing notwithstanding affliction;

Adjusting and flourishing, notwithstanding misfortune, is a vital part of individual and expert development. When faced with difficulties, people and associations frequently track down ways of advancing and succeeding. Here are some few articles issues to consider:

Versatility: Flexibility is the capacity to return quickly from misfortunes. Creating versatility is essential for adjusting to misfortune. This includes remaining hopeful, keeping an uplifting outlook, and learning from failures. Flexibility: Being versatile means being open to change and novel thoughts. Embracing change can assist people and organizations with tracking down imaginative answers to problems. Learning and Development: Difficulty frequently presents amazing open doors for learning and self-awareness. While confronting tough spots, individuals can acquire new abilities, information, and experiences that can help them over the long haul.

Critical thinking: Adjusting to misfortune requires compelling critical thinking abilities. Breaking down difficulties, distinguishing arrangements, and making a move are fundamental stages in beating deterrents.

Emotionally supportive networks: Building serious areas of strength for an organization of companions, family, coaches, or partners can offer close-to-home and functional help during difficult stretches.

Care and taking care of oneself: Rehearsing care and taking care of oneself can assist people with managing pressure and keeping up with their prosperity in testing circumstances.

Arranging and Arrangement: Being proactive by expecting possible difficulties and having emergency courses of action set up can make it more straightforward to adjust when affliction strikes.

Embracing Change: At times, misfortune is an impetus for fundamental change. Embracing change as a chance for development can prompt improved results.

Imagination and Advancement: Misfortune frequently starts inventiveness and development. It can prompt the advancement of new items, administrations, or ways to deal with critical thinking.

Ingenuity: Diligence is key when confronting affliction. Proceeding to pursue objectives, even notwithstanding mishaps, can prompt

possible success. In synopsis, adjusting and
flourishing despite difficulty is tied in with
building versatility, being available to
change, gaining from difficulties, and
keeping a positive outlook. A cycle includes
both individual and expert turns of events,
and it can prompt more prominent strength
and progress over the long haul.

Chapter 6

Analyzing sound and viable survival techniques that advance strength:

In this part, we will investigate the idea of flexibility and dive into the different sound and compelling methods for dealing with especially difficult times that can help people fabricate and keep up with versatility despite life's difficulties. Strength is the capacity to return quickly from misfortune, adjust to change, and develop further through troublesome encounters. Looking at these survival methods is fundamental to improving one's close-to-home prosperity and the general nature of life. Understanding Flexibility: Versatility is certainly not a proper quality but instead a unique expertise that can be created and reinforced over the long haul. It includes the ability to oversee pressure, defeat misfortunes, and keep an uplifting perspective even notwithstanding difficulty. Versatile people will generally have better mental and actual wellbeing, more grounded connections, and a more significant level of by and large life fulfillment.

Solid survival methods:

Social Help: Building and keeping areas of strength for an organization of loved ones can give a pivotal foundation to versatility. Conversing with believed people and looking for their help during testing times can be monstrously useful.

Profound Guideline: Figuring out how to recognize, express, and deal with feelings in a sound way is fundamental. This incorporates exercises like care, reflection, and profound breathing activities that can assist with controlling close-to-home reactions.

Critical thinking Abilities: Creating compelling critical thinking abilities empowers people to handle difficulty with a proactive outlook. It includes separating issues into sensible advances and looking for arrangements.

Versatile Reasoning: Developing a development mentality and reevaluating negative considerations can prompt more hopeful and tough reasoning examples. This can be accomplished through mental social procedures and positive self-talk.

Actual Prosperity: Dealing with one's actual wellbeing through standard activity, a fair eating routine, and adequate rest is central to flexibility. A solid body upholds a sound mind. Seeking Proficient Assistance: There is no disgrace in looking for help from emotional well-being experts while adapting to overpowering difficulties. Treatment and guidance can provide important devices and backing.

Keeping a Feeling of Direction: Having an unmistakable feeling of direction and objectives in life can give inspiration and direction in any event, even during extreme times. Adaptability: Strong people are, in many cases, versatile and open to change. They can change their procedures and assumptions because of changing conditions.

Powerful survival methods: The adequacy of ways of dealing with hardship or stress can shift from one individual to another and circumstance to circumstance. It means quite a bit to explore different avenues regarding various methodologies and design them to your novel requirements and conditions. Furthermore, building strength is a continuous cycle that requires practice and self-awareness. By inspecting and carrying out these sound and powerful ways of dealing with especially difficult times, people can encourage versatility, which assists them with exploring difficulties as well as prompts a seriously satisfying and fulfilling life. Please let me know if you'd like more unambiguous data or have any inquiries connected with this subject!

Examining critical thinking abilities, looking for help from others, and using positive self-talk as instances of versatile ways of dealing with stress:

Versatile methods for dealing with especially difficult times are vital for managing difficulties and stress. Here is a conversation on three such components: critical thinking abilities, looking for help from others, and using positive self-talk.

Critical thinking Abilities: Critical thinking abilities include recognizing and settling issues intelligently. When confronted with an issue, people areas of strength for tackling abilities separate it into reasonable parts, put forth objectives, and methodically make progress toward arrangements. For instance, on the off chance that somebody is battling with a weighty responsibility, they could make a plan for the day, focus on undertakings, and designate time effectively. This assists in diminishing focusing as well as lifting certainty and self-viability.

Looking for Help from Others: Looking for help from companions, family, or experts is another compelling survival strategy. At the point when individuals share their difficulties and sentiments with others, they frequently gain new viewpoints and everyday reassurance. This can be especially useful during difficult stretches. For example, somebody managing an individual misfortune might track down comfort in conversing with a guide or trusting in a confided-in companion. The demonstration of connecting can lighten profound weights and encourage a feeling of association.

 Using Positive Self-Talk: Positive self-talk includes intentionally changing negative considerations into additional valuable and hopeful ones. At the point when people take part in pessimistic self-talk, they frequently amplify issues and sabotage their capacity to adapt. Interestingly, positive self-talk supports an outlook of flexibility and self-conviction. For example, rather than thinking, "I can't deal with this," somebody could say, "I'll approach it slowly and carefully; I've overcome difficulties previously." This change in speculation can work for profound prosperity and reinforce confidence. Adaptive survival strategies like critical thinking, looking for help, and positive self-talk enable people to explore life's troubles with flexibility. By integrating these procedures into their adapting tool compartment, individuals can upgrade their general prosperity and better oversee the stressors they experience.

Final summary

Far in excess of adapting" alludes to a mentality and way to deal with managing difficulties that goes beyond the run-of-the mill techniques for adapting. It includes finding proactive ways to address stressors, embracing strength, and looking for self-awareness. This approach urges people to oversee tough spots as well as use them as open doors for personal growth and advancement. It frequently includes looking for help, growing new abilities, and keeping an uplifting perspective even in the face of misfortune. Far in excess of adapting is tied in with flourishing, not simply getting by, in that frame of mind of life's difficulties.

Far in excess of Adapting" proposes a subject connected with outperforming or surpassing the standard techniques for managing

difficulties or hardships. It probably
investigates methodologies or approaches
that go beyond simple adaptation to
accomplish improved results or self-aware
Looking